Hooked on Aromatherapy
Non-Toxic Beauty & Cleaning Recipes

By Debbie Kameka

What is Aromatherapy?

Aromatherapy has been around as an ancient practice that started approximately 6,000 years ago where essential oils were extracted from plants and flowers and used as a way of healing and for medical benefits.

Essential oils can be used to enhance your mood, manage pain, sleep, overall wellness and boost your immune system. You can use essential oils topically on your skin to penetrate the body and go through all the organs and systems in the body. You can also inhale or smell the essential oils. By inhaling three deep breaths the aroma will travel through the nose hairs and up to the limbic system. The limbic system connects with the part of the brain that controls mood, emotions, feelings and memories. This instantly triggers the brain to release chemicals to help the body relax.

Plants and flowers have been around for thousands and thousands of years, they have been resilient to many microbes, bacteria and virus' thus making them very anti-fungal, anti-bacterial, anti-inflammatory and anti-oxidant. The purest source you will find. Essential oils offer a very natural response for the body to release endorphins which are the feel good chemicals in your body.

Did you know that we absorb up to 60% of what we put on our skin?

This causes us to have a higher risk of disease as we age when we are exposed to toxins on a daily basis. Many products that we use on a regular basis contain toxic and carcinogenic ingredients. By eliminating some of these toxins your body's organs can perform properly instead of the constant detoxing process to try to eliminate them.

Here is a list of a few toxic ingredients and preservatives found in skin care and beauty products you should try to avoid:

Benzoyl Peroxide: can be found in acne products, also toxic by inhalation.

DEA, MEA & TEA: Diethanolamine, Momoethanolamine & Triethanolamine are foam boosters and is easily absorbed through the skin and accumulates in the body organs and the brain.

Dioxin: This compound will not appear in list of ingredients but it is often found in antibacterial ingredients like triclosan, emulsifiers, PEG's and ethoxylated cleansers like Sodium Laureth Sulphate. Dioxin is reported to cause cancer.

DMDM Hydantoin & Urea: These preservatives release formaldehyde which may cause joint pain, cancer, allergies, depression, headaches, chronic fatigue, dizziness and insomnia.

FD&C Color: Contain heavy metal salts that deposit toxins in the skin. Absorption can cause depletion of oxygen. If the product is with color it will have FD&C. Animal studies show almost all are carcinogenic.

Parabens: Methyl, Butyl, Ethyl, Propyl these preservatives are not always labeled but are found in deodorants and other skin care products.

PEG: Polyethylene Glycol has dangerous levels of Dioxin have been found as a by-product of the ethoxylation process. PEG is found in deodorant and most personal care products, baby products and sunscreen.

Phthalates: Not usually listed on the label but found in many products. Health effects include damage to liver, kidneys and birth defects.

Propylene Glycol: Along with Butylene Glycol are petroleum plastics. PG is considered so toxic it requires gloves. Clothing, goggles and disposal by burying. Furthermore, EPA warns against skin contact to prevent brain, liver and kidney malfunctions.

Sodium Lauryl Sulfate: Also Sodium Laureth Sulfate is used in toothpaste and 90% of personal care products that foam. Also used in car washes, garage floor cleaners and engine degreasers. Prolong use can cause eye damage, depression, labored breathing, skin problems and death.

Avobenzone: Benzphenone, Ethoxycinnamate, PABA are chemicals in sunscreen. These ingredients have been reported to be free radical generators and are believed to damage DNA and lead to cancer.

Triclosan: This antibacterial ingredient found in soaps registers with the EPA as a pesticide also classified as a chlorophenol which is suspected in causing cancer in humans.

Natural Home Cleaning Recipes

Lavender-Lemongrass Liquid Dish Soap

1 Natural Unscented Glycerin Soap Bar
3 cups Boiled Water
1/2 cup 100% Pure Vegetable Glycerin
30 Drops Lavender Pure Essential Oil
20 Drops Lemongrass Pure Essential Oil

Start by using a cheese grater to shred the glycerin soap bar to make ½ cup shredded soap. You may use a clear vegetable glycerin soap bar or if you cannot find that bar you may use an Ivory soap bar.

1. Add the shredded soap and boiling water together in glass bowl and stir until the soap is dissolved. If the soap does not dissolve completely you can place the glass bowl in a pot with an inch of water and heat it on low. Stir the soap mixture until completely dissolved. Let sit 5 minutes.

2. Stir in the 100% Pure Vegetable Glycerin and the Lavender and Lemongrass pure essential oils. Mix well.

3. Allow the mixture to cool. If your mixture gets any lumps stir with a wire whisk or fork until smooth. Pour into a bottle and it is ready for use.

Lavender-Lemon Liquid Hand Soap

1/2 cup finely grated Natural Glycerin Soap Bar
5 cups water
1/2 tablespoon Vegetable Glycerin
1/2 teaspoon (2 capsules) Vitamin E
20 drops Lavender Pure Essential Oil
10 Drops Lemongrass Pure Essential Oil

1. Grate the soap bar using the fine side of your cheese grater, the larger the flakes the less smooth your soap will turn out.

2. Add the grated soap, water and vegetable glycerin into a large pot and cook over low heat until the soap has melted. Stir to a thin consistency and make sure there are no soap lumps that have not dissolved.

3. Let the mixture cool overnight or 12 hours. Once the mixture is cooled it will look milky and lumpy.

4. Using an electric hand mixer or egg beater, whip the homemade liquid soap mixture until it becomes smooth.

5. Stir in the Vitamin E, Lavender and Lemongrass oils. Pour the soap into dark glass, ceramic or PET plastic soap bottles and use as normal. Keep any extra in a large glass bottle in a cool dark place.

Eucalyptus Anti-Bacterial Hand Soap

1/2 cup finely grated Natural Glycerin Soap Bar
5 cups water
1/2 tablespoon Vegetable Glycerin
1/2 teaspoon (2 capsules) Vitamin E
25 drops Peppermint Pure Essential Oil
15 drops Orange Pure Essential Oil
5 drops Eucalyptus Pure Essential Oil
5 drops Rose Geranium Essential Oil

1. Grate the soap bar using the fine side of your cheese grater, the larger the flakes the less smooth your soap will turn out.

2. Add the grated soap, water and vegetable glycerin into a large pot and cook over low heat until the soap has melted, stir to a thin consistency. Let the mixture cool overnight or 12 hours. Once the mixture is cooled it will look milky and lumpy.

4. Using an electric hand mixer or egg beater, whip the homemade liquid soap mixture until it becomes smooth. Stir in the Vitamin E and the Pure Essential Oils.

5. Pour the soap into dark glass, ceramic or PET plastic soap bottles and use as normal. Keep any extra in a large glass bottle in a cool dark place.

You can control the consistency of your homemade liquid soap by changing the amount of water you use. For a thinner, runnier liquid add more water. Experiment until you get the thickness you want.

Eucalyptus Glass & Mirror Cleaner

¼ cup Vodka
1/3 cup White Vinegar
1 1/2 cups Distilled Water
10 Drops Eucalyptus Pure Essential Oil

Combine white vinegar and vodka with distilled water in a spray bottle. Add Eucalyptus Oil. Shake well.

To Use: Spray onto mirror or glass surface and wipe off with newspaper or a micro fiber cloth.

Tea Tree Heavy Duty Window Glass Cleaner

For tougher jobs try this recipe

1 Cup Distilled Water
1 Cup White Vinegar or Vodka
¼ teaspoon Liquid Dish Soap
5 Drops Lemon Pure Essential Oil
5 Drops Tea Tree Essential Oil
5 Drops Lavender Essential Oil

1. Combine water and white vinegar or vodka with 1/4 teaspoon liquid dishwashing soap in a spray bottle.

2. Add lemon, tea tree and lavender essential oils. Shake well.

To Use: Spray on and wipe off with newspaper or lint-free cloth.

Orange-Bergamot All Purpose Cleaner

1 teaspoon Borax
1/4 cup White Vinegar or Vodka
2 cups Distilled Water
15 drops Orange Pure Essential Oil
15 drops Bergamot Pure Essential Oil

1. Boil the water. Pour water into a large glass measuring cup or pitcher with a spout.

2. Add the borax and stir until dissolved. Add the vinegar or vodka. Let cool and then pour the mixture into a spray bottle. Add the essential oils to the spray bottle.

Here are a few other variations you can try:

Anti-Bacterial
10 drops each eucalyptus, peppermint and orange essential oils.

Anxiety-Free Cleaning
10 drops each rosemary, lavender and lemon essential oils.

Lemon Sparkle
20 drops each lemongrass and tea tree essential oils.

Bathtub Scrub Cleaner

This is a powerful scrub for the tub. Removes soap scum, water deposits and disinfects too.

1/3 cup Washing Soda
1/3 cup Baking Soda
1 teaspoon Virgin Coconut Oil
5 drops Eucalyptus Pure Essential Oil
5 drops Lemongrass Pure Essential Oil

Mix the Washing Soda and Baking Soda in small dish. Stir in coconut oil until blended. Add Essential oil and mix well.

To Use: Sprinkle in tub or sink and scrub, then rinse away.

Cinnamon & Spice Grout Cleaner

Whiten and brighten your grout with the power of spice. Kills mildew-causing fungi and lifts deep down dirt.

1/2 cup Borax
1/2 cup Baking Soda
1/3 cup Vodka
1 teaspoon Virgin Coconut Oil
5 drops Cinnamon Bark Essential Oil
5 drops Clove Essential Oil
5 drops Tea Tree or Thyme Essential Oil

1. Mix all ingredients together until they make a smooth paste.

2. Use a grout brush, scrub the mixture into the grout and let sit for at least 15 minutes, then rinse.

You may want to wear gloves this blend can irritate the skin.

Natural Lemon Cleaner
for Toilet Bowl Ring

1 cup Borax
¼ cup Lemon Juice

1. Pour Borax and Lemon Juice into the toilet bowl.

2. Let sit overnight. In the morning, scrub with a toilet brush, then flush to rinse.

Tip: For tough stains, remove some of the water out of the toilet to expose the ring, then rub the paste into the ring and let stand overnight. In the morning, scrub once more then flush to rinse.

Grapefruit Heavy Duty Floor Cleaner

This is one of the best homemade kitchen floor cleaners, removes sticky messes, stains, mud tracks, grease and it also works well on other floors surfaces.
No rinsing necessary.

Bucket of Hot Water
½ cup Vodka
¼ cup Baking Soda
15 drops Grapefruit Pure Essential Oil

1. Fill a bucket with hot water.
2. Add Baking Soda, stir until dissolved
3. Add Vodka and Grapefruit Oil

Mop or sponge clean your floor surface ceramic tile, vinyl, laminate, granite and hardwood floors.

Natural Lavender Carpet Fresh

2 cups Baking Soda Sifted
10 drops Lavender Pure Essential Oil
5 drops Lemongrass Pure Essential Oil
5 drops Rosemary Pure Essential Oil
Shaker Jar (see cover)

1. Mix all ingredients well and place in a covered container overnight so the oils can be absorbed.

2. Sprinkle a fine layer of homemade carpet cleaner and leave on to absorb odors for a while then vacuum thoroughly. This can be used every time you vacuum and is safe for your pets.

Citrus Stainless Steel Sink Scrub

Removes stains, brightens and shines stainless steel and disinfects too.

1/3 cup Borax
1/3 cup Baking Soda
1 teaspoon Virgin Coconut Oil
5 drops Orange Pure Essential Oil
5 drops Lemongrass Pure Essential Oil

Mix all ingredients together in a small plastic container.

Lemon–Eucalyptus Powder Dishwasher Detergent

This simple homemade dishwasher soap cleans without toxic chemicals. It works best if you rinse heavily soiled dishes first.

1 cup Baking Soda
1 cup Borax
10 drops Lemon OR Lemongrass Essential Oil
10 drops Eucalyptus Essential Oil

!. Mix together the baking soda and borax in a plastic container.

2. Stir in the Essential Oils and mix until blended.

To Use: Add 2 to 4 tablespoons to your dishwasher's soap compartment.

Lemon Grapefruit Dishwasher Rinse Aid

Boost your dishwasher's cleaning power by adding rinse aid to the rinse compartment before you run the dishwasher. This treatment also keeps your dishwasher fresh and running clean.

1 cup White Vinegar
10 drops Lemongrass Essential Oil
10 drops Grapefruit Essential Oil

Combine all ingredients and store in a plastic bottle. Add the rinse aid to the rinse compartment before washing.

Tip: To clean your dishwasher, fill the rinse compartment and run the dishwasher on a normal cycle, this will remove odors and any residue inside your unit. You can even use this rinse aid on your hand washed dishes. Just add a couple tablespoons to your rinse water and dip your dishes for the final rinse.

Baking Soda-Vinegar Drain Cleaner

Use this recipe once a week to keep your kitchen sink free from soap and grease residues that can build up and block your drain. Do not store this recipe in a container, it is meant to be used in the drain immediately.

1 cup Baking Soda
1 cup Distilled White Vinegar
Boiling Water

1. Pour a pot of boiling water down the drain.

2. Pour ½ cup baking soda in the drain, let sit a few minutes.

3. Pour 1 cup Vinegar in the drain. The solution will start to bubble. Use a drain plug if you have one to keep the solution from backing up.

4. Let sit for 5-10 minutes, and then flush with another pot of boiling water.

Garbage Disposal Freshener

Make and store this recipe for weeks of citrus freshness

Quartered Orange or Lemon Peels
White Vinegar

1. Take the quartered citrus peels and place in a jar. Fill the jar with vinegar and store for 2 weeks. Shake container every day to mix.

2. After 2 weeks, you can use a ½ cup of the vinegar straight in the garbage disposal with a couple of citrus peels to freshen and a few ice cubes to clean the blades.

The smell of the vinegar will be replaced by the citrus scent. Try this recipe with grapefruit, lemon and orange.

Powdered Lavender-Lemon Laundry Soap

2 cups Soap Flakes (see directions below for making soap flakes)
1 cup Washing Soda
1 cup Borax
½ c. Baking Soda
20 drops Lemon or Lemongrass Pure Essential Oil
20 drops Lavender Pure Essential Oil

1. To make soap flakes, grate a bar of unscented clear natural glycerin soap using the fine side of your cheese grater, the finer you make the soap the better. If you cannot find this soap you may use any natural colored soap such as organic goat's milk soap.

2. Combine all the ingredients in a large airtight container. Stir to combine or just put the lid on and shake vigorously.

To Use: Add 2 tablespoons to your washer per load.

Tea Tree Aloe Hand Sanitizer

1 cup Pure Aloe Vera Gel
1 tablespoon Witch Hazel
30 drops (1/4 tsp) Tea Tree Pure Essential Oil
10 drops Lavender Pure Essential Oil
3-4 drops Vitamin E Oil
1 teaspoon Vegetable Glycerin

Mix together the essential oils and Aloe in a re-usable pump bottle if you have one. Add the witch hazel, vegetable glycerin and vitamin E oil and mix well.

Organic Homemade Hand & Body Lotion

1/2 cup Pure Almond Oil
1/4 cup Organic Virgin Coconut Oil
1/4 cup Beeswax
1 teaspoon Vitamin E Oil
2 Tablespoons Shea Butter or Cocoa Butter
10-15 drops Pure Essential Oil

1. Combine ingredients in a shallow jar. Fill a medium saucepan with a couple inches of water and place over medium heat.

2. Put a lid on the jar loosely and place the jar in the pan with water.

3. As the water heats, the ingredients in the jar will start to melt. Shake or stir occasionally to blend the mixture. When all ingredients are completely melted, pour into whatever jar or tin you will use for storage. Small mason jars are great for this.

Use as you would regular lotion. This has a longer shelf life than some homemade lotion recipes since all ingredients are already shelf stable and not water is added.

Use within 6 months for best moisturizing benefits.

Eucalyptus-Peppermint Antibacterial Wipes

16 oz. Homemade Hand & Body Lotion (recipe found here)
16 oz. Rubbing Alcohol (1 Bottle)
10 drops Eucalyptus Essential Oil
10 drops Peppermint Essential Oil
Heavy duty paper towels
Plastic Container for the finished wipes

1. Add Lotion, Rubbing Alcohol and Essential Oils in a large Ziplock bag or container. You will need to kneed or stir this mixture to be fully blended.

2. Cut the paper towels into 3 pieces; make sure they stay attached at their perforation so they pull out of the container one by one.

3. Place the cut paper towel pieces in your container and pour the liquid over it. Allow it to sit for at least 30 minutes so it will soak up all the liquid. Rotate the container to completely saturate the towels.

4. Cut a slit in the lid to have access to your wipes if you like.

Tea Tree Spray for Mold

2 teaspoons Tea Tree Pure Essential Oil
2 cups Water

Combine ingredients in a spray bottle, shake to blend, and spray on problem areas. Do not rinse. Let it dry on. As the formula dries it will kill the mold.

Nothing natural works for mold and mildew as well as this spray and the Tea Tree Oil leaves a lasting scent of aroma in the room.

Peppermint Toilet Bomb

1 cup Baking Soda
1/2 cup Citric Acid
20 drops Lavender Essential Oil
20 Drops Peppermint Essential Oil
10 drops Eucalyptus Essential Oil
ice cube tray
Spray Bottle with Water

1. Add the baking soda to a mixing bowl and use a fork to break up any clumps. Add the citric acid and mix very well.

2. Add the essential oils and gently mix. Spray lightly with water just enough to mist, stir gently. Mist and stir a couple more times. Mixture should look dry and clumpy but not wet.

3. Pack mixture very well into ice cube tray to make your bombs. Let dry for at least four hours or overnight. After the bombs have hardened remove from ice cube tray and store in jar with lid.

TIP: You can add a few drops of food coloring to the water bottle to give your bombs a little color.

To Use: Drop one bomb in the toilet as needed to freshen the bowl. This will leave a nice scent in your bathroom too.

Outdoor Furniture Cleaner

2 cups White Vinegar
10 drops Rosemary Essential Oil
10 drops Eucalyptus Essential Oil
10 drops Lemon Essential Oil

Combine all ingredients in a spray bottle and spray directly on the areas with mold, do not rinse. Straight vinegar reportedly kills 82% of mold.

Calming Lavender Room Spray

4 oz. Purified Water
1 t. Vegetable Glycerin
80 drops Lavender Pure Essential Oil
Small Spray Bottle

Fill a small 2 – 4 ounce spray bottle with Purified Water and add 80 to 100 drops of Lavender essential oil.

Shake well before each use as ingredients will separate.

Real Orange Wood Polish

2 tsp. Olive Oil
1 cup White Vinegar
10 drops Orange Pure Essential Oil

Mix together these ingredients and store in airtight bottle or jar.

To Use: Shake well and apply to a rag or soft cloth and polish wood surfaces and furniture. Conditions and restores wood leaving a nice shine.

Real Orange Candle

This clever candle can be made easily with oranges, grapefruits or lemons.

1 Orange
½ cup Olive Oil
20 drops Lemongrass Essential Oil

1. Cut orange in half and scoop out pulp leaving the stem in the center.

2. Fill the orange with Olive Oil but do not overfill and cover the stem. Add Lemongrass Oil.

3. Light "wick", it takes a few tries as the stem is moist once the heat from the fire draws the oil up the stem it will light and burn for hours.

To Use: Do not leave lit orange unattended and it's best to place your lit orange in a small dish or bowl as it is burning.

Laundry Stain Booster

1 cup Purified Water
1/2 cup Hydrogen Peroxide
1/2 cup Washing Soda
Dark Spray Bottle

1. Mix all ingredients together and store in a dark spray bottle. (Hydrogen peroxide loses its effectiveness if stored in a light container)

2. To use, spray on laundry stains and let it sit overnight or for a few hours. If you need to soak a large load of clothes you can double the recipe and soak clothes overnight, then launder as usual.

Peppermint Granite Cleaner

1/4 cup Rubbing Alcohol or Vodka
3 drops of Dawn or other dish soap
Purified Water
10 drops Peppermint Pure Essential Oil
Spray Bottle

1. Put the rubbing alcohol or vodka into a 16 oz spray bottle

2. Add the Dish Soap and Peppermint Oil

3. Fill up the rest of the bottle with water.

To use, spray on granite surface and wipe dry with a soft cloth. This formula leaves no greasy residue behind and makes your granite shine streak free.

Lavender Fabric Softener

1/2 cup Baking Soda
4 cups Purified Water
3 cups White Vinegar
10 drops Lavender Pure Essential Oil
Plastic Bottle

1. Add the baking soda to your plastic bottle plus 1 cup of warm water stir until the baking soda is dissolved.

2. Then add the remaining 3 cups of water to the bottle

3. Very slowly add the white vinegar, there will be a reaction with the baking soda, try to avoid the liquid from flowing out of the bottle

4. Add the Lavender essential oil

Use as you would normally by adding a small cup to your washer's fabric softener compartment.

Eucalyptus-Lemon Leather Furniture Cleaner

1/2 cup Olive Oil
1/4 cup White Vinegar
10 drops Eucalyptus Essential Oil
10 drops Lemon Essential Oil
Spray Bottle

1. Add Olive Oil to spray bottle.

2. Add White Vinegar and Essential oils, shake well

To use, shake well with each use and spray directly onto leather or vinyl surface. Use a soft cloth to wipe down and condition your leather furniture and vinyl surfaces.

This is great to use on leather furniture, spa covers, saddles or inside your car.

Scented Lace Curtain Brightener

Remove yellowing from lace curtains or tablecloths

2 cups 3% Hydrogen Peroxide
20 drops Geranium Essential Oil
Water

1. Fill a sink with cold water, Geranium Oil and 2 cups of Hydrogen Peroxide.

2. Soak for at least an hour, rinse in cold water and air dry.

Grapefruit Bathroom Spray

1/2 cup Vodka
1 cup Distilled Water
1 T. Grapefruit Pure Essential Oil
Spray Bottle

Mix together all ingredients into spray bottle and spray on any surface in your bathroom from mirrors, sink, vanity, shower walls, fixtures, toilets and floors.

This leaves a fresh clean citrus scent all around the room.

Lavender Aromatherapy Pillow Spray

2 oz. Purified Water
2 oz. Vodka
20 drops Lavender Essential Oil
Spray Bottle

Combine ingredients in spray bottle. Shake well before each use.

Spray as needed to pillow and bedding prior to bedtime.

Calms and relaxes you naturally making it easier to fall asleep.

Skunk Odor Remover

1 quart 3% Hydrogen Peroxide
¼ cup Baking Soda
1 T. Liquid Dish Soap
20 drops Tea Tree Essential Oil

Mix ingredients together and spray on effected areas.

Lemon Dishwasher Powder

3 cups Washing Soda
1 cup Baking Soda
10 drops Lemon Pure Essential Oil

1. Add all ingredients to a glass container with lid and shake well to mix.

2. Use 2 Tablespoons of the mixture and add it to the soap compartment of your dishwasher.

If you notice a spots on your glasses reduce the amount of the mixture to 1 ½ Tablespoons. See the recipe to use for the homemade rinse aid too.

Rosemary-Lemon Oven Cleaner

½ – ¾ cup Salt
¼ cup Washing Soda
1 box (16oz) Baking Soda
¼ cup Water
¾ cup White Vinegar
10 drops Rosemary Pure Essential Oil
10 drops Lemon or Lemongrass Pure Essential Oil
Spray Bottle

1. Remove oven racks and preheat oven to 250 degrees for 15 minutes. Turn off oven and leave the door open.

2. Mix together salt, washing soda and baking soda in a glass bowl.

3. Add enough water to create a paste.

4. Carefully spread the paste on the oven walls with a sponge and allow to set for 20-30 min.

5. Mix together the vinegar and essential oils in a spray bottle. Shake well then spray the oven walls and wipe clean with a damp sponge or cloth.

Aromatherapy Shoe Deodorizer

4 T. Baking Soda
4 T. Cornstarch
6 drops Tea Tree Pure Essential Oil
6 drops Lavender Pure Essential Oil
6 drops Eucalyptus Pure Essential Oil

1. Combine the cornstarch and baking soda together in a bowl.

2. Add the essential oils, and stir. Store in an airtight container until ready to use.

To Use: Sprinkle the deodorizer lightly into shoes into dry shoes and let sit overnight. Before wearing, tap on the soles to eliminate and discard the excess powder from the interior of the shoes. Repeat as needed.

Homemade Eucalyptus Sink Scrub

Great for stainless steel sinks, porcelain sinks & tubs.

½ cup Baking Soda
1 ½ oz. Vegetable Glycerin (approx. 8 T.)
20 drops Eucalyptus Pure Essential Oil

1. Stir together ½ cup Baking Soda and Vegetable Glycerin until blended.

2. Add Eucalyptus oil and stir. Store in tub.

To Use: Scoop the mixture onto a sponge and scrub the surface. This mixture has a soft abrasive to remove stuck on food and soap scum rings in the tub. Washes away clean. Some separation of ingredients may occur, stir before use.

Microwave Your Aromatherapy

Eliminate fish and cooking smells instantly and freshen the room

1 cup water
5-6 drops Lemongrass Pure Essential Oil

Fill a bowl with 1 cup water and 5-6 drops lemongrass oil.

Cook for 5 minutes in your microwave.

You can use this recipe anytime you want to freshen your home, try with Lavender Oil, Rose Absolute Oil or Sandalwood.

As a bonus this also will clean and freshen your microwave, the steam lifts stuck on food. Simply wipe down with a damp sponge.

Orange Glass Top Stove Cleaner

½ cup Water
¼ cup White Vinegar
10 drops Orange Pure Essential Oil
Spray bottle

Mix all ingredients together in spray bottle.

To Use: Spray mixture onto glass stove top and wipe dry with a clean soft cloth.
Cuts grease and leaves no residue behind.

Glass Stove Top Cleaner for Baked On Mess

½ cup Baking Soda
¼ cup Water
5 drops Rosemary Essential Oil
5 drops Tea Tree Essential Oil

1. Mix together the baking soda and water to make a paste and then stir in the essential oils.

2. With a spoon cover the affected baked-on areas with the mixture. Let sit for 5-10 min.

3. Using a scrub sponge in a circular motion to remove the baked on grease. Wipe clean. A scraper may also be used to loosen and lift the mess.

Lavender Scented Lightbulbs

Use this recipe with any of your favorite scents

Lavender Pure Essential Oil

Put 5-6 drops of Lavender on a cotton ball and wipe down your light bulbs when not in use. When you turn on your light again the heat from the bulb will warm the oil and add a nice fragrance to your room.

Precaution: Make sure the light bulb is off and cold before adding the essential oil.

TIP: You can also add a few drops of essential oil to the cardboard of the toilet paper roll for added scent in your bathroom.

Eucalyptus
Gel Air Freshener in a Jar

1 oz. Gelatin, powdered
2 cups Water, divided
20 drops Eucalyptus Essential Oil
1 T Salt
food coloring to tint the air freshener
Small Jars

1. Bring one cup of water to a boil in a small saucepan. Add gelatin to the boiling water and stir until smooth and dissolved.

2. Add the salt and the second cup of cold water and whisk. Set aside.

3. Add Eucalyptus oil and food coloring to the jar(s).

4. Quickly pour the hot liquid gelatin over the essential oil mixture. Stir. Allow mixture to cool, uncovered.

When it reaches room temperature,
place where ever you want a nice scent.
Gel freshener should last about four weeks.

Bergamot
Wood Scratch Remover

½ cup White Vinegar
½ cup Olive Oil
10 drops Bergamot Essential Oil

Mix all ingredients together and massage into affected areas.

Homemade Liquid Laundry Soap

1 bar of natural soap
1 cup Borax
1 cup Washing Soda
2 empty gallon jugs/containers

1. Grate your bar of soap into a large pot and fill one gallon jug with water and pour into pot with grated soap.

2. Cook until the grated soap dissolves. Add the Borax and Washing Soda. Bring to a boil. It will coagulate.

3. Turn off the heat. Add 1 gallon of cold water. Stir well. Cool. Fill gallon containers using a funnel.

To Use: ¼ cup per load, for more soiled laundry you may use ½ cup of laundry soap.

Lemongrass-Grapefruit Dishwasher Detergent Pods

2 cups Washing Soda
½ Baking Soda
1 T. Lime Juice
20 drops Lemongrass Pure Essential Oil
30 drops Grapefruit Pure Essential Oil
1/2 cup of White Vinegar
2 Ice Cube Trays

1. Add Washing Soda and Baking Soda into a mixing bowl.

2. Add the Essential oils and Lime Juice into the bowl with dry ingredients. Stir.

3. Pour the vinegar into the bowl slowly, stirring as you add. The vinegar will cause the mixture to bubble.

4. Stir your mixture, it should be a little moist so that you will be able to press it down and mold it into the ice cube trays.

5. Spoon into ice cube trays and pack firmly. Let them harden for 24-48 hrs. Remove from ice trays and store in air tight jar. Use 1 pod per load.

This recipe filled 1 ½ ice cube trays.

Tea Tree Oil
Sticky Label Remover

¼ cup Canola Oil
10 drops Tea Tree Essential Oil
Hair Dryer

Mix together the Canola Oil and Tea Tree Oil. Apply the mixture on the label with a cloth and saturate.

Heat the label with a low setting of the hair dryer then use a scrubby pad to remove the sticky residue.

Follow up with soap and water to remove the oils and remaining particles.

Aroma-Yoga Mat Cleaner

1/3 cup water
1/4 cup witch hazel
10 drops Tea Tree oil
5 drops Peppermint oil
5 drops Eucalyptus oil
5 drops Lavender oil
Spray Bottle

Combine all ingredients in a spray bottle and store in a dark area when not in use.

To use, spray all over the surface of your yoga mat. Take a damp cloth and wipe dry. Repeat on the other side, and let air dry for 10 minutes.

Pooper Spray

Use this spray pre-business to cut back on odor

10 drops Lemongrass Essential Oil
10 drops Grapefruit Essential Oil
10 drops Bergamot Essential Oil
10 drops Eucalyptus Essential Oil
4 ounces of water
Spray bottle

Fill the spray bottle with 4 ounces of water and add all of the Essential Oils.

Shake the bottle and spray into the toilet bowl pre-business. Approximately 3 or 4 sprays should do. The oils will disperse over the water creating a vapor barrier and trapping any offensive odors.

Natural Skin & Body Care

Coconut-Citrus Scalp Treatment

Stimulates the blood circulation and loosens any dry skin scales

4 Tablespoons Coconut Oil
4 drops Tea Tree Essential Oil
4 drops of Rosemary Essential Oil
2 Tablespoons Fresh Lemon Juice
1 Tablespoons Fresh Grapefruit Juice

1. Stir Coconut Oil until smooth then add remaining ingredients and blend well.

2. Apply to dry hair starting on the top and separate hair by parting and continue to apply mixture throughout the scalp. Make sure the mixture covers the entire scalp.

3. Now give your scalp a good massage. Rub with your fingertips in a circular motion all over the scalp. Leave the treatment on for about 20 minutes.

Finish it off with a good shampoo and conditioner.

Fresh Peppermint Mouthwash

1 cup Purified Water
1 teaspoon Baking Soda
5-10 drops Peppermint Essential Oil
Small glass container

Mix all ingredients in a glass jar and shake well.

To Use: Swish in mouth and then spit out.

After-Shower Lavender Oil Spritz

4 oz. Grapeseed Oil
4 oz. Sweet Almond Oil
15 drops Lavender Essential Oil
Spray Bottle

Mix all ingredients together and spray on wet skin and massage in.

Cooling Aloe After-Sun Spray

4 oz Aloe Vera gel (or pulp from fresh aloe plant)
15 drops Lavender essential oil
1 oz Vitamin E Oil
5 drops Eucalyptus Essential Oil
5 Tbsp Witch Hazel
5 Tbsp Water
4 oz. Spray Bottle

1. Mix together Aloe Gel, Vitamin E, and the Essential oils in a jar or small bowl.

2. Add in the witch hazel and water and stir to blend. Pour into spray bottle and store in the refrigerator.

To Use: After a day in the sun, shake well and spray affected areas.

Will keep for 1-2 months in the refrigerator

"Amazing Grace" Natural Deodorant

2 T. Coconut Oil
1 T. Baking Soda
3 Tb. Arrowroot Powder
5 drops Amazing Grace Fragrance Oil
2 oz. plastic tub or jar
1 cosmetic sponge pad

1. Mix together Coconut Oil, Baking Soda and Arrowroot Powder until blended.

2. Add Amazing Grace fragrance oil and stir then put into the container.

To Use: Apply after showering to non-broken skin by applying with a cosmetic sponge or fingertips and massage in.

Organic Banana Face Mask

1 egg yolk
1 mashed Organic Banana
1 teaspoon Olive Oil
1 teaspoon Coconut Oil
1 teaspoon Honey

1. Mix together egg yolk, mashed banana, olive oil until well blended.

2. Add coconut oil and honey and stir until well blended.

To Use: Apply to clean dry face and let set for 20 mins. Rinse with cold water and pat dry. Moisturize if needed.

Overnight Lemon Sun Spot Lightener

2 oz. Apple Cider Vinegar
2 oz. Fresh Lemon Juice
5 drops Lemon Essential Oil
4 oz. container
Cotton pads

Mix together all ingredients in the container.

To Use: Apply mixture to a cotton ball and soothe all over face as a toner. It is normal to experience a little redness or stinging at first (just like you would with a toner). If you have sensitive skin, or if it feels too strong dilute with water.

For best results do not rinse, leave on overnight.

Peppermint-Wintergreen Toothpaste

7 Tbs. Calcium Magnesium Powder
4 Tbs. Coconut Oil
1 Tbs. Baking Soda
3 Tbs. Distilled Water
40+ drops Peppermint Essential Oil
20+ drops Wintergreen Essential Oil

Mix all ingredients in a mini-food processor and mix well to incorporate or use a whisk/fork in a bowl. Store in a small jar.

To Use: as you would regular toothpaste.

Pre-Brush Teeth Whitener

1 oz. Baking Soda
1 oz. Hydrogen Peroxide
10 drops Peppermint Essential Oil

1. Mix together Baking Soda and Hydrogen Peroxide into a smooth paste.

2. Add Peppermint oil and blend.

To Use: Dip your toothbrush in the paste and brush for about 2 minutes before brushing.
Follow up with natural toothpaste

Orange-Lavender Hairspray

1 organic Orange – for dark hair
1 organic Lemon – for light hair
2 cups Distilled Water
2-3 Tbs. Vodka
6-8 drops Lavender Essential Oil
Spray bottle

1. Cut a whole orange or lemon into wedges and combine with 2 cups water in a small pot. Boil over medium high heat until liquid is reduced by half.

2. Strain liquid through cheesecloth into a measuring cup. If you boiled too much liquid out add water until you have 1 cup. Allow citrus juice to cool.

3. Combine alcohol and essential oils in a small bowl, swirl to mix, then add to the cup of citrus juice.

4. Use a funnel to pour into a spray bottle with a fine mister and shake to combine ingredients. Shake before each use.

Orange Massage Oil for Cellulite

2 oz. Grapeseed Oil
2 oz. Almond Oil
2 capsules Vitamin E Oil
1 Tsp. Coconut Oil
10 drops Orange Essential Oil

1. Mix together the Grapeseed Oil and Almond Oil in a small bowl.

2. Break open the capsules of Vitamin E Oil and add to the oil mixture. Blend.

3. Stir in the Coconut Oil and orange Oil til blended. Pour into small bottle to store.

To Use: Massage into affected area regularly.

Brown Sugar Body Polish

1 Cup Brown Sugar
¼ Cup Almond Oil
1 Tsp. Coconut Oil
2 capsules Vitamin E Oil
10 drops Eucalyptus Essential Oil

Mix together all of the ingredients and store in a tub with a lid.

To Use: It is best to use this scrub in the shower for all over body and feet treatment. Massage all over to exfoliate dead skin. Leaves skin feeling ultra soft and moisturized. Draws out toxins from the skin and aromatizes the shower.

Homemade Almond-Zinc Sunscreen

1/2 cup Almond Oil
1/4 cup Coconut Oil
1/4 cup Beeswax
2 Tbs. Zinc Oxide- Be careful not to inhale the powder
1 tsp. Vitamin E oil
2 Tbs. Shea Butter

1. Combine all ingredients except zinc oxide in a pint sized or larger glass jar.

2. Fill a medium saucepan with a couple inches of water and place over medium heat. Put a lid on the jar loosely and place in the pan with the water.

3. As the water heats, the ingredients in the jar will start to melt. Shake or stir occasionally to incorporate. When all ingredients are completely melted, add the zinc oxide, stir in well and pour into whatever jar or tin you will use for storage.

Best if used within six months. This sunscreen is not completely waterproof and will need to be reapplied after sweating or swimming.

This recipe has an SPF of about 20.

"Amazing Grace" Natural Perfume Oil

1 oz. Baobab Oil
2 drops Bergamot Essential Oil
5 drops Amazing Grace Fragrance Oil
2 drops Frankincense Essential Oil

Add essential oils to baobab oil and mix thoroughly. Store in a small vile or perfume bottle. Dab a drop or two onto wrists, neck, behind ears and massage into skin with fingertips.

Other Perfume Blends:

9 drops Grapefruit Essential Oil
1 drop Rose Geranium Essential Oil
1 drop Ylang Ylang Essential Oil

6 drops Lavender Essential Oil
4 drops Frankincense Essential Oil
1 drop Rose Geranium Essential Oil

8 drops Sandalwood Essential Oil
2 drops Orange Essential Oil
1 drop Patchouli Essential Oil
1 drop Ylang Ylang Essential Oil

Homemade Vanilla Body Butter

1/4 cup Cocoa Butter
1 cup Shea Butter
3 Tbs. Grapeseed Oil
1 Tbs. Jojoba Oil
1/4 tsp. Vitamin E Oil
1 tsp. Corn Starch
30 drops Vanilla Absolute Essential Oil

Mix all ingredients together and store in a glass jar or tub. Massage into skin as needed.

De-Stressing Aromatherapy Bath Oil

2 oz. Jojoba Oil
2 oz. Almond Oil
30 drops Lavender Essential Oil
2 drops Chamomile Essential Oil
2 drops Clary Sage Essential Oil
2 drops Rose Geranium Essential Oil
2 drops Cypress Essential Oil
Bottle

Combine all the ingredients and put in bottle.

To Use: Pour about a tablespoon into a warm bath after you've finished running the water.

Aloe Vera Hair Growth Serum

Great for thinning hair

1/4 cup Aloe Vera gel
1 tsp. Jojoba Oil
12 drops Lavender Essential Oil
10 drops Rosemary Essential Oil
3 drops Cedarwood Essential Oil
Plastic bottle

Combine all of the ingredients in a plastic bottle and shake lightly to mix.

To Use: Massage 1 tablespoon of the mixture into your scalp each night before going to bed. Massage your scalp for at least 15 minutes to increase blood flow to the scalp, release tension, stimulate hair follicles and help the treatment penetrate more deeply.

Detoxing Sea Salt Body Scrub

10 drops Lemon Essential Oil
10 drops Eucalyptus Essential Oil
10 drops Grapefruit Essential Oil
5 drops Rosemary Essential Oil
1 cup Sea Salt
2 T. Almond Oil
1 t. Coconut Oil

1. Combine Sea Salt, Coconut Oil and Almond Oil in a bowl and stir until well blended.

2. Add the Essential Oils and stir until blended. It should have a dry flakey consistency.

To Use: Massage into your skin while in the shower to exfoliate the skin.

Hot Jojoba Oil Restorative Hair Treatment

2 Tbs. Jojoba Oil
6 drops Sandalwood Essential Oil
3 drops Chamomile Essential Oil
1 drop Ylang Ylang Essential Oil

(One Treatment)

1. Combine all ingredients in a small glass and put the glass into a bowl of very hot water. Stir the hot oil mixture until it feels very warm.

2. Apply the hot oil straight onto your dry hair or dampen your hair slightly.

3. Pile your hair on top of your head and put on a shower cap or wrap your hair in plastic wrap. Wrap a towel around your head and relax for at least 20 minutes. Then wash hair as usual.

Peppermint Foot Cream

5 oz. Shea Butter
2 oz. Coconut Oil
40 drops Peppermint Essential Oil
20 drops Tea Tree Essential Oil

Mix in all the ingredients together and massage in tired feet as needed.

Lavender Spray Deodorant

1/4 cup Witch Hazel
1/4 cup Aloe Vera Gel
1/4 cup Purified Water
1 tsp. Vegetable Glycerin
20 drops Lavender Essential Oil

Mix together all the ingredients in a spray bottle. Shake to blend, and spray on as needed.

Detoxing Foot Scrub

Revive tired feet and eliminate toxins with this aromatherapy foot scrub.

2 cups Sea Salt
2 T. Almond Oil
2 T. Grapeseed Oil
2 T. Pine Oil
2 T. Patchouli Oil
2 T. Chamomile Oil
2 T. Geranium Oil
1 T. Coconut Oil
Vitamin E Oil from 2 capsules
10 drops Lemon Pure Essential Oil
10 drops Eucalyptus Essential Oil
10 drops Grapefruit Essential Oil
10 drops Rosemary Essential Oil
10 Drops Peppermint Oil

1. Add Sea Salt and oils and stir until well blended.

2. Add all essential oils and mix well. Store in tub or jar with lid.

To Use: Soak feet in warm water for a few minutes to open pores. Then apply detox scrub to feet and massage in for a few minutes then rinse feet and pat dry.

Peppermint-Eucalyptus Cooling Spray

Great on hot summer days

2 oz. Witch Hazel
1 oz. Distilled Water
50 drops Peppermint Essential Oil
15 drops Eucalyptus Essential Oil

Mix all ingredients in a spray bottle, shake before use and apply to your neck for instant cooling relief.

Cooling Hot Flash Oil

10 drops Lemon Essential Oil
10 drops Peppermint Essential Oil
10 drops Clary Sage Essential Oil
10 drops Lavender Essential Oil
10 drops Geranium Essential Oil
2 oz. Jojoba Oil

Mix all ingredients and dab or spray on wrists, face or neck when you feel a hot flash coming on.

For Night Sweats

2 oz. Purified Water
1 oz. Witch Hazel
10 drops Peppermint Essential Oil

Combine all ingredients in a spray bottle and keep next to your nightstand to use as needed at night.

Organic Hair Conditioner

1 cup Organic Coconut Oil
1 teaspoon Vitamin E Oil
1 teaspoon Jojoba Oil
5 drops Lavender Essential Oil
5 drops Cedarwood Essential Oil
5 drops Rosemary Essential Oil

Place all ingredients in a mixing bowl. Mix on high for 3 minutes. Transfer into a container.

To Use: Wash hair as usual and apply to dampened hair, massage in and leave on hair for 2 minutes and rinse.

Miracle Eye Cream

2 T. Coconut Oil
2 tsp. Almond Oil
2 Vitamin E Oil capsule

1. Fill your container with coconut oil and almond oil. Stir until blended.

2. Pierce the vitamin E capsules and add to the coconut oil mixture.

To Apply: Cleanse the eye area. Use a spatula to remove a small amount of eye cream not to contaminate your mixture. Apply lightly under the eye area, at the sides and over the eyelids. This is a great night cream but can also be worn under make-up.

Grapefruit-Lavender Body Spray

10 drops Grapefruit Essential Oil
10 drops Lavender Essential Oil
2 oz. Purified Water
3 drops Vegetable Glycerin
1 Spray Bottle

Combine all ingredients in spray bottle.
Shake well and spray.

Geranium Citrus Cuticle Cream

1 tsp. Virgin Olive Oil
2 oz. Shea Butter
1 tsp. Vegetable Glycerin
4 Vitamin E Oil Capsules
10 drops Lemongrass Essential Oil
10 drops Orange Essential Oil
Geranium Essential Oil
Rosemary Essential Oil

1. Mix together Olive Oil, Shea Butter and Vegetable Glycerin.

2. Pierce the Vitamin E capsules and add oil to the mixture and blend. Add Essential Oils.

To Use: Massage into cuticles each night, throughout the day, or whenever needed for intense moisturizing.

Strengthening Nail Oil

2 T. Vitamin E Oil (or 10 capsules)
10 drops Frankincense Essential Oil
10 drops Myrrh Essential Oil
10 drops Lemon Essential Oil

Mix the ingredients together and store in a dark colored bottle.

To Use: Rub on nails twice a week.

Creamy Lemon Night Cream

1 tsp Organic Coconut Oil
2 T Almond Oil
1/2 T Organic Shea Butter
1 tsp Vitamin E oil
2 T Grape Seed Oil
5-10 drops Lemon Pure Essential Oil

Mix ingredients together and store in airtight jar.

To Use: Soothe on face and neck in upward motion before bedtime.

Leave-in Citrus Hair Conditioner

2 T water soluble Almond Oil
1 T Coconut Oil
5 oz. Purified Water
5 drops Orange Essential Oil
4 drops Lemon Essential Oil
2 drops Grapefruit Essential Oil
2 drops Rosemary Essential Oil

Combine all ingredients in a plastic spray bottle.

To Use: Spray on damp, clean hair and massage or brush in. Style as usual.

Soothing Eucalyptus Foot Powder

2 Tbsp Baking soda
4 Tbsp Cornstarch
1/4 tsp Orris Root Powder
15 drops Eucalyptus Essential Oil
10 drops Spearmint Essential Oil

1. Mix essential oils with Orris root powder.

2. Add a small amount of the mixture to the baking soda and cornstarch until blended. Store in an air tight container.

To Use: Sprinkle on feet and lightly rub. Sprinkle inside shoes to freshen.

Zit Destroyer Oil

3 T. Jojoba Oil
8 drops of Lavender Essential Oil
4 drops Tea Tree Essential Oil
3 drops Cypress Essential Oil
2 drops Helichrysum Essential Oil

Mix all oils together in a container.

To Use: Add a few drops to a cotton swab and dab on each acne spot. Do not use this oil mixture on your entire face. Use on acne spots several times a day.

Lavender Lemon Nail Growth Serum

20 drops Lavender Essential Oil
10 drops Lemon Essential Oil
2 T Almond Oil
Vitamin E Oil from 2 capsules

Add all oils to a bottle and shake to blend.

To Use: Massage oil on the nail bed once a day to encourage healthy growth and give nails a shear look and feel. If nail fungus is present add 5 drops Tea Tree Oil to mixture.

Booty Spray

Use post bathroom or anytime you want to freshen up.

2 oz. Witch Hazel
2 oz. purified Water
5 drops Vegetable Glycerin
10 drops Lavender Essential Oil

Combine all ingredients in a small spray bottle and shake well.

To Use: Shake well before use and spray on toilet paper and use as needed.

Natural First-Aid Recipes

Headache Relief Oil

20 drops Peppermint Essential Oil
10 drops Lavender Essential Oil
5 drops Eucalyptus Essential Oil
5 drops Rosemary Essential Oil
5 drops Ylang Ylang Essential Oil
1/4 cup Almond Oil

Mix all ingredients together in small bottle and apply to temples and forehead as needed.

Organic Eczema & Dermatitis Cream

2 T. Organic Coconut Oil
3 oz. Avocado Oil
5 oz. Organic Pure Shea Butter
10 drops Lavender Essential Oil
10 drops Tea Tree Essential Oil

Mix ingredients together and blend for 5 minutes on the "whip setting". Store in small tub or jar.

Do a patch test on your skin before applying all over.

If using this recipe on a child start out with only 5 drops each of Essential Oils.

To Use: Apply directly to affected areas as often as needed.

Muscle Relieving Body Rub

10 drops Rosemary Essential Oil
10 drops Eucalyptus Essential Oil
5 drops Lavender Essential Oil
Vitamin E Oil from 2 Capsules
2 oz. Almond Oil

Mix and apply to muscles before or after exercise.

Chest Congestion & Sinus Recipe

10 drops Lemon Essential Oil
10 drops Tea Tree Essential Oil
20 drops Eucalyptus Essential Oil
Humidifier
Water

To Use: Add all ingredients in basin of the humidifier to relieve congestion and stuffiness.

Cold Sore Ointment

1 t. Coconut Oil
5 drops Lavender Essential Oil

Mix together and apply directly to cold sore.

Peppermint
Fever Cool Down Oil

2 T. Almond Oil
10 drops Peppermint Essential Oil

Mix together and apply to the bottoms of your feet and apply with cloth to back of the neck.

Calming Cough Oil

¼ c. Almond Oil
10 drops Spearmint Essential Oil
10 drops Eucalyptus Essential Oil

Mix together and massage into chest as needed.

Homemade Honey Cough Syrup

3 T. Lemon Juice
¼ c. Raw Honey
2T Coconut Oil

To Use: Take 1-2 T. as needed

Sleep-Aid Massage Oil

20 drops Lavender Essential Oil
10 drops Sweet Marjoram Essential Oil
10 drops Vetiver Essential Oil
2 oz. Grapeseed Oil

Mix all ingredients and massage into temples before bedtime.

Sore Feet Treat

10 drops Geranium Essential Oil
20 drops Lavender Essential Oil
20 drop Peppermint Essential Oil
2 oz. Almond Oil

Mix all ingredients together in a small bottle.

To Use: Massage small amount into tired feet. Alternatively add the blend to a bowl of warm water and soak the feet for 10 minutes and then pat dry.

Head Lice Hair Treatment

10 drop Eucalyptus Essential Oil
10 drop Lavender Essential Oil
20 drops Tea Tree Essential Oil
½ c. Sunflower Oil

Mix ingredients together in a small bottle

To Use: Massage a good amount into the scalp. Cover hair with a plastic shower cap or plastic bag and leave on for an hour or overnight.

Shampoo out the next morning - rub the shampoo in before adding water to get rid of the greasiness of the oil.

As a preventative measure add 5 drops of Tea Tree Essential Oil and 5 drops of Lavender Essential Oil to 1 tsp of mild shampoo and use to shampoo hair.

Afterword & Dedication

I hope this book has brought some awareness of the toxins that are in so many products that we use daily and you will be inspired to create your own products to increase your quality of health and life. Keeping our bodies healthy is the greatest gift you can give to yourself and your family. I wish you much joy and success as you continue your journey in Aromatherapy.

I dedicate this book to my mom, Bonnie for her support of me and my ideas and helping them come to life. She is my icon as a homemaker and has such a creative talent for decorating and designing almost anything she touches. I also want to thank my husband, Desmond and my son, Desi who never complained as I spent hours on end writing this book and turning our kitchen into an experimental lab.

Many thanks and gratitude,
Debbie Kameka

Precautions

Contents contained herein should go with the understanding that all ingredients listed must be used at the user's own discretion. Author or publisher shall not be held responsible for any damages to property or for any adverse physical effects, including injury or bodily harm caused by insufficient knowledge or the improper use of any ingredient or reaction to an essential oil. As with any new process, a small scale testing for evaluation purposes prior to full use is recommended. Pregnant women, small children or if there is a cat in the home should use extra caution and limit use to pure essential oils. Consult your physician prior to using essential oils if you are under a physician's care.